MW01379703

Thirty Questions

A SHORT CATECHISM ON THE CHRISTIAN FAITH

If you find this book helpful, join our work at Seedbed
by sowing it into the life of another. Give it away. More copies
are available, print and electronic, at Seebdbed.com.

While there, subscribe to our weekly briefing, read articles daily,
and browse the growing library of resources.

Seedbed

Sowing for a Great Awakening

Thirty Questions

A SHORT CATECHISM ON THE CHRISTIAN FAITH

TIMOTHY C. TENNENT

seedbed
PUBLISHING

seedbed.com

Copyright 2012 by Timothy C. Tennent

All rights reserved. Written permission must be secured from the publisher to use or reproduce any part of this book, except for brief quotations in critical reviews or articles.

Printed in the United States of America

16   15   14   13   12   1   2   3   4   5

Library of Congress Control Number:

ISBN: 978-1-62171-007-3

Cover and page design by Haley Hill
Cover photo courtesy of Wikipedia.

Unless otherwise indicated, all Scripture quotations are taken from HOLY BIBLE, NEW INTERNATIONAL VERSION®. Copyright © 1973, 1978, 1984 by International Bible Society. Used by permission of Zondervan. All rights reserved.

Scripture quotations marked ESV are taken from the Holy Bible: English Standard Version, copyright © 2001, Wheaton: Good News Publishers. Used by permission. All rights reserved.

Scripture quotations marked NASB are taken from the New American Standard Bible®. Copyright © 1960, 1962, 1968, 1971, 1972, 1973, 1975, 1977, 1995 by The Lockman Foundation. Used by permission.

SEEDBED PUBLISHING
Sowing for a Great Awakening
204 N. Lexington Avenue, Wilmore, Kentucky 40390
www.seedbed.com

Dedicated to the memory of Susanna Wesley (1669–1742), who was the twenty-fifth child in her family, and became the mother of nineteen children. Few could match her deep commitment to catechesis. It is from her that her sons John and Charles first learned the faith. Her own catechesis which she wrote on the Apostles' Creed, Lord's Prayer, and Ten Commandments was lost in the famous fire when the rectory burned down but her fifteenth child, John Wesley, was miraculously rescued and became her "brand plucked from the burning." It is fitting that today she bears the title "Mother of Methodism."

Contents

Introduction

Christians in the Western world have enjoyed a long sojourn at the center of cultural life. For hundreds of years we could expect that, broadly speaking, Judeo-Christian values were held up as worthy of emulation. People may not have followed the Ten Commandments, but they believed that they were *true* and that they reflected how people *should* live. Christianity was widely regarded as setting forth the proper moral standard for society. Christian values were generally defended in the church, in the home, and in society.

Today, Christianity in the Western world is in the diminishing sunset of that kind of relationship with the surrounding culture. Christian values are no longer defended in society, are not taught in most homes and, surprisingly, are even being questioned in some churches that have lost the courage to teach the Christian faith with reasonable clarity. Our society increasingly doubts that truth is even knowable or that ultimate truth exists. The Bible is viewed as an antiquated and contradictory book with a questionable moral framework.

There is a growing distrust in institutions and authority, whether the government or the church. Religion in general, and Christianity in particular, is often viewed as a shrill, disruptive voice in society, associated more with bigotry and anger than sound values, godly character, and wise counsel for life, not to mention a message of forgiveness and eternal life. A recent national campaign by atheists produced billboards across the nation with a picture of Jesus and the words: "Sadistic God, useless Savior, 30,000+ versions of 'truth', promotes hate, calls it love." We also live in a period of skepticism about the reliability of historical narratives, whether the iconic account of George Washington crossing the Delaware or Luke writing his gospel. As Christians, we must recognize that the Western world is entering a post-Christian phase which requires a far more deliberate effort to pass down the faith in an intentional way to our children and, indeed, for all of us to understand the basic framework of Christian thought better. In short, we need a rebirth of catechesis.

The word "catechesis" means "to sound down." It refers to a teaching exchange between a seasoned, secure Christian and a new believer. The church has invested enormous time and energy into catechesis all through history. Small manuals were produced which were used to teach the basics of Christian faith. They were often in question-and-answer format and generally covered the Ten Commandments, the Lord's Prayer, the Apostles' Creed, the nature of the church, and the sacraments. There were longer manuals which were used by the church in confirmation classes and shorter manuals which were used by parents at home. All of the Protestant churches which emerged in the sixteenth century produced catechesis manuals. John Wesley's first encounter with the Christian faith would have been through an Anglican catechism which he learned from his mother, Susanna, who became widely known for her deep commitment to the catechesis of children—not only her own children, but many others as well.

Today, the pace of contemporary life, the exponential rise of time spent in entertainment, and the "light-weight" relational-oriented format of many Sunday school programs, youth groups, and worship services has left us with a whole generation of Christians who have only the vaguest idea as to what Christians actually believe. When pressed by an increasingly skeptical, even hostile generation, Christians are often unable to articulate their faith. Furthermore, because the church itself has not been immersed in a Christian worldview, the moral and ethical life of the church is slowly beginning to conform to the surrounding culture.

The purpose of this meditation is to provide a thirty-day short course in the Christian faith. Like traditional catechesis manuals, it is organized in a question-and-answer format. The questions can be used as a morning or evening devotional during any month of the year. Alternatively, a church or small Bible study group can use the manual over an eight-week period as follows: Week 1, questions 1–3; Week 2, questions 4–6; Week 3, questions 7–11; Week 4, questions 12–15; Week 5, question 16; Week 6, questions 17–20; Week 7, questions 21–25; and Week 8, questions 26–30.

Traditional catechesis manuals pose a question and then provide a short, pithy one-sentence reply. In this catechesis a more lengthy explanation is given which invites discussion, reflection, and interaction. The Apostles' Creed, the Ten Commandments, and the Lord's Prayer are included in this manual's appendices. These three selections should be memorized by the individual or the group during the month meditation or during the eight-week study. It is recommended that each day or session begin with a reading of the Apostles' Creed and the Ten Commandments and close with the Lord's Prayer. Throughout the meditation there are passages of Scripture which support the answer. These texts can be read to supplement the meditation and aid discussion as an integral part of the study.

The church has been sustained for nearly two thousand years through a careful commitment to catechesis. By engaging in this study, you are joining with millions of Christians over the ages who not only believed the faith, but learned it, remembering the final command of Jesus to "*teach* them everything I have commanded you" (see Matt. 28:20), as well as the words of Peter who said, "In your hearts set apart Christ as Lord. Always be prepared to give an answer to everyone who asks you to give the reason for the hope that you have. But do this with gentleness and respect" (1 Pet. 3:15).

Thirty
Questions

1

Who is God?

God is a personal being, infinite in love, knowledge, and power. He is perfect in wisdom, goodness, righteousness, justice, holiness, and truth. God is both the creator and sustainer of the universe. He is the final goal and judge of the universe, infinite and perfect in all his attributes.

The Jewish/Christian understanding of God is unique among all the religions of the world. Hinduism remains uncertain whether we can know that God is personal, or infinite in his perfections. Islam affirms that God is infinite in his perfections, but is uncertain if God can be personally knowable. Buddhism is officially nontheistic, denying all first causes, including God. In contrast, Christians affirm that God is personal *and* knowable.

To say that he is perfect in all his attributes is to declare that every attribute of God is enjoyed by him in its perfect state. He is infinitely pure, infinitely holy, infinitely righteous, infinitely loving, and so forth. Because we only know these attributes in fragmentary and distorted ways, we cannot fully comprehend how all these attributes are held perfectly and infinitely by God. Sometimes we may look at circumstances and not be able to discern how the justice or the love of God is manifest in certain situations. We do find comfort, however, in knowing that in the end, we shall see him as he truly is, and that he will make all things right. In the meantime, we can put our full trust and confidence in God's nature and character.

If you ever go to London you will probably visit Trafalgar Square. It is in the heart of the city and is a well-known tourist attraction. The most prominent feature in the square is Nelson's Column. It is a tribute to Lord Nelson's sea victory over the combined fleets of the French and Spanish Navy in 1805. Although Nelson died in the conflict, the British fleet prevailed and this victory confirmed the superiority of the British navy. The problem is that the statue of Nelson is so high above the square (170 feet) that no one can see what he looked like. He is high and exalted above the square, but he is also removed from the people.

This is analogous to the Christian proclamation about God. He is exalted above all creation. He is perfect in his attributes. But until Christ came we could not fully understand or know what God is like. The Christian view is that in Christ—and only in Christ—is the glory of God known or understood. In Christ, God came down and lived among us, showing us his life and character in intimate detail. In the face of Christ the full glory and grace of God has been made known.

Scripture Reading

1 Chronicles 29:10–13
2 Chronicles 20:6
Job 42:2

Psalm 90
Isaiah 44:6
1 Corinthians 1:30

2

How do we know what God is like?

God has made himself known to us in acts of personal self-disclosure. This self-disclosure occurs in two major ways, known as general revelation and special revelation. General revelation refers to all the ways God has universally made himself known to all people in all places and in all times. General revelation, sometimes called natural or universal revelation, has occurred in two major ways. Those two ways are outwardly through the created order and inwardly in the universal presence of human conscience. First, God reveals his presence, character, and attributes through the created order. Through creation we understand that God is a God of order, beauty, and power.

Second, God reveals his presence and moral character through the presence of human conscience. Even though there are areas where people differ about what is right or wrong, the very presence of the *categories* of right and wrong demonstrate that we live in a moral order. Even young children demonstrate deeply imbedded notions of fairness and longings for justice, and we teach them to "be kind" as a virtue we instinctively value. When someone murders or steals, we all can testify to a sense of "wrongness." Likewise, when someone acts sacrificially to help or serve another person or creature, they have a sense of "rightness" about such actions. All this testifies to the presence of a moral order.

Special revelation refers to all the ways God has made his nature and purposes known specifically to certain people at particular times, but which are not universally known. Special revelation also occurs in two major ways. The first is through the revelation of Holy Scripture. God has revealed his will, his character, and his purposes to specific people throughout time, and this revelation has been recorded in the Bible. This includes his mighty acts of deliverance, his miraculous interventions, and the specific revelation of his moral character, as in the Ten Commandments revealed to Moses on Mount Sinai. The second is through the revelation of God's Son, Jesus Christ. As noted in the previous meditation, it is through the incarnation of Jesus Christ that we come fully to understand who God is, his saving purposes, and his love.

It is through the ongoing work of the Holy Spirit that the purpose and will of God is applied to the life of the church and the individual believer. In the gospel of John it is declared that "no one has ever seen God; the only God, who is at the Father's side, he has made him known" (John 1:18 ESV).

Christianity is unique because in Christ, God seeks to reveal himself (not just his will). One of Islam's greatest theologians, Al-Ghazali, famously declared that Allah does not reveal himself, he only reveals his will. In Christianity, we discover that God not only reveals his will, but he also seeks to reveal *himself* and calls us to know him in a personal way.

Scripture Reading

Psalm 19

John 14:9–11

Romans 1:18–20

Romans 2:12–15

2 Timothy 3:16

Hebrews 1:1–2

Hebrews 4:12

3

What is the Trinity?

Christianity, like all monotheistic religions, asserts that there is only one God. We do not believe in three Gods. However, Christianity is unique in our understanding that the one God exists in three eternal and personal distinctions known as Father, Son, and Holy Spirit. The church has used the word "Trinity" to capture this great mystery. The word "Trinity" is a combination of two words, "Tri" and "unity." The "tri" refers to the three eternal distinctions; the "unity" is to reinforce that we believe in only one God. This is normally expressed by saying that we believe that God is one in essence, but reveals himself through three eternal personal distinctions known as Father, Son, and Holy Spirit.

The purpose of this revelation is primarily to demonstrate the personal, relational nature of God. God is, even apart from creation, eternally personal and relational. As the Puritans once observed, "God is, in himself, a sweet society." There is relationship in the very nature of who God is. The whole universe flows forth from an eternal, relational tri-unity, not from a non-relational, solitary figure as taught by Islam.

The Christian idea that internal differentiation does not contradict God's unity is even testified to in the created order. For example, a stone has little internal differentiation and, therefore, is not particularly unified in essence. If you split a stone into two pieces, you have not destroyed the essence of the stone, you have only created two smaller stones. However, if you cut a tiger into two pieces you do not get two small tigers, you get one dead tiger! Some of the lower creatures can be severed into two parts and still live and move independently for some time. Because their differentiation is low, their unity is likewise low. The more conscious and intelligent a being is, the greater the differentiation and the more profound the unity.

A person possesses a mind, thoughts, and speech. We function as a unity despite internal distinctions. The same point could be made about the body, soul, and spirit of a person. The fact that God himself has internal differentiation does not contradict his unity. On the contrary, we observe this harmony of plurality and unity in all higher forms of life.

The nature and essence of God is admittedly complex and mysterious. A common misunderstanding of God is that he took different forms at different times in history, but could only be in one form at any given time. This, however, is not a proper understanding of the Trinity. The three distinctions are co-existent, co-eternal, and equal. God decided in his self-revelation that the best way for humans to understand him is to see him as one God, revealed as Father, Son, and Holy Spirit. These three are not three separate modes, or operations, but three eternal relations within the One true God, the Trinity.

Scripture Reading

Genesis 3:6

Genesis 17:1

Psalm 46:10

Isaiah 44:6

Matthew 28:18–20

John 1:1

John 1:34

John 10:30

John 20:28

Acts 5:3–4

Romans 9:5

1 Corinthians 2:9–16

2 Corinthians 3:17

2 Corinthians 13:14

2 Thessalonians 1:12

Titus 2:13

1 Peter 1:1–2

2 Peter 1:1

4

Did God create the world and the human race?

The Scripture reveals that God created the heavens and the earth in all its vast array. He created all things visible and invisible. There is nothing in the entire universe, including space and time, which does not have its origin in God's being and creative acts. God is the first cause of everything. Christians have long distinguished between immediate and mediate creation. Immediate creation means that God creates directly "out of nothing." He spoke and matter was created. He spoke and order was brought out of chaos, and so forth. God also creates in mediate ways, meaning that he superintends the ongoing creative overflow of the world. This means that God not only started everything by creating time, space, and matter, it also means that he continues to superintend his creation even as we participate with him in creation through childbearing and other kinds of creative acts, including everything from painting a portrait to designing a rocket to creating an electronic circuit for cell phones and personal computers.

While all Christians believe, in principle, in both immediate and mediate creation by God, there are genuine differences about where the line is drawn. Some Christians have a very broad view of mediate creation which would include an extended evolutionary process in the emergence of the current created order. Other Christians reject most evolutionary theories and believe that the entire created order, in all its detailed intricacies, is the result of the immediate act of God's spoken word. Certainly no truly Christian view, however, can deny that God is the first cause of the universe, that he created man and woman in his own image, and that he is sovereign over all of creation, including a direct supervision of the whole creation. God created the world out of nothing by calling it into existence.

Although Deism affirms that God created all that is, it digresses from Christianity by maintaining that God then left the world to "run on its own," and that he does not superintend or involve himself any further in its operation or supervision. Jesus, however, said that not even a sparrow falls to the ground without his knowing. The Old Testament declares that God charts the course of the thunderbolt. All of Scripture bears witness that God is our Good Shepherd, who cares for and watches over us as an attentive shepherd takes care of his flock. These statements are meant to convey that God is intimately involved in his creation and is not an absentee owner disinterested in his creation.

Scripture Reading

Genesis 1:1

Genesis 14:19

Deuteronomy 10:14

Nehemiah 9:6

Psalm 23

Isaiah 40:28

John 1:1–3

John 10:11–15

Colossians 1:16–17

Hebrews 11:3

Revelation 4:11

5

What does it mean that we are created "in the image of God"?

The Scripture reveals that the created order emerged out of the spoken word of God. However, when God created man and woman, we are told that we were fashioned out of the dust of the earth and that he breathed into us the breath of life. We were "created in his own image." We should not understand that the "image of God" means that we physically look like God or that God has a physical body like us. The Scripture declares that "God is spirit" (John 4:24).

The idea that we are "created in the image of God" generally refers to three distinct capacities which have been granted to the human race. The first is a spiritual capacity. This means that we are meant to reflect his nature in the world. The image of God is like a mirror. We are to "mirror" or "reflect" God's character and presence in the world. We are to reflect his holiness, his righteousness, his love, his creativity, and so forth. Indeed, we are to reflect every attribute of God which can possibly be communicated to a finite person. The second feature of the image of God is relational. We have the capacity to know God and to communicate with him. We also have capacities for relationships with one another which are profound and glorious. We can truly love God and our neighbor. Finally, the image of God grants us the capacity to represent God in the world. We are his ambassadors in the world. We are to govern the world and share in his rule and reign over it. God always remains sovereign over the universe, but he has delegated the care and nurture of the earth to us. We are commanded to fill the earth, rule over it, care for it, and subdue it for his glory and our good.

Scripture Reading

Genesis 1:26–27
1 Corinthians 15:49
2 Corinthians 3:17–18

6

What is the purpose and meaning of life?

One of the most well-known catechisms in Christian history declared that the purpose of our existence is to "love God and to enjoy him forever." It is one of the most famous and powerful statements about the purpose of life. If we only live for ourselves and our own enjoyment, we experience a nagging sense that we have somehow missed the final purpose of life. We are meant to know God in his beauty, power, love, and majesty. We are meant to find fulfillment and meaning in orienting our lives towards his greater purposes for us and for creation as a whole. There is no greater purpose in life than being bearers of the image of God in the world. Our personal lives have meaning as they are caught up in God's grand plan and purpose for the universe. He is reconciling all things to himself—so we are ambassadors of reconciliation. He is the author of all creation—so we share in his creativity. He is the source of all life and hope—so we become bearers of that life and hope in the world. All lasting meaning and purpose is ultimately derived from him and his unfolding purpose and plan for the entire creation which, in time, will give birth to the new heavens and the new earth, where all things fully acknowledge his sovereign rule and reign.

One of the marks of our age is the increasing despair and hopelessness which seems to shroud so many in our time. However, the root problem is not that we have too much anxiety, but too little hope. Hope, along with faith and love, is one of the abiding and sustaining qualities of the Christian. We are people of hope.

Scripture Reading

Proverbs 19:21
Romans 15:20–21
Ephesians 1:3–14

7

What is sin and how did it enter into the human race?

Sin is all the ways we rebel against God and resist his work in the world. However, sin is not ultimately rooted in our disobedience to a set of commandments. Sin is, at its root, the sign of a broken relationship. We were created to live in perfect harmony with God and our neighbor. Sin manifests itself in a wide array of broken relationships—with God, with our neighbor, and even with creation itself. In one way or another, sin is rooted in putting ourselves first, resulting in our inability to properly love God and our neighbor.

According to Scripture, the first man, Adam, was a representative man and had the capacity to either love and serve God as he was created to do, or to rebel against him. We might wonder why God gave such a choice to Adam. God could have created Adam without a free will. However, we all know even from our own experience with relationships that people with power and position can make us obey them, but cannot force us to love them. Love is one of the greatest capacities we have, but it is rooted in free will and choice. We have already demonstrated that God created us in his own image and desired that we have a relationship with him rooted in love. However, this cannot be possible unless we also have the freedom to go our own way, reject God, and pursue our own path. For love to be the nature of our relationship with God, it must be freely chosen.

Adam chose to disobey God and rebelled against him, asserting his own will in place of God's will. This is known as the Fall of Man. The reason Adam's disobedience was so grave and his sin is known as the Fall of Man (not merely the Fall of Adam), is because Adam acted as a representative man on behalf of the entire human race. The Scriptures teach that when the one man Adam sinned, sin spread to the entire human race. It was like a virus on a computer system which spreads to the entire network. We are now born with a sin nature and a natural bent towards sin. There is a classic saying about this which every Christian should learn. It goes like this: *"We are not sinners because we sin, we sin because we are sinners."* Adam's rebellion made us sinners and we are now born with a sin nature. In a thousand ways we confirm Adam's sin in our own lives by our own sinning. However, we must not forget that our sins are the result of the presence of sin which has been unleashed into the world. Children do not have to be taught to disobey or to be angry or selfish. They must be taught to obey, to share, to love, and so forth. We all know which way the twig is bent. The depravity of humanity is probably the most experientially provable doctrine of Christianity.

It may, at first, seem unfair, but, as we will explore later, God provides another representative man, Jesus Christ. He becomes our Second Adam, and through his one act of obedience makes us righteous in the same way that Adam acted and made us sinners. In Christ, all our broken relationships are restored and all the effects of sin are reversed. The last symbol of sin is death itself, and in Christ, even that is overturned. In the resurrection at the end of time our bodies will be raised and all the effects of sin will finally be defeated. What a great hope we have, knowing that the formidable enemy of sin has been vanquished and eventually all its spoils will be lost.

Scripture Reading

Genesis 3:1–19
Romans 5:12–21

8

Why did God call Abraham and enter into a covenant with Israel?

After humanity fell in the Garden of Eden and entered into rebellion, God began to unfold a plan of redemption. It involved two key features.

First, God called a people to himself, entered into a covenant with them, and revealed his righteousness to them. The purpose of the covenant was to enter into a committed relationship with people and reveal his faithful love. The Fall, as noted earlier, is rooted in broken relationships. A covenant is, in contrast, a relationship which is steadfast. Even in the midst of a sinful world, all of us long for those who are committed to us to be faithful. We long for relationships to not be broken. We long for people to keep their promises. God shows us how this can be done. In fact, even when the people of God broke the covenant and sinned against God, he remained steadfast, faithful, and true.

Second, even though God began with one people, he revealed to that people his wider saving purposes and his desire to bless all the peoples and nations of the world. Abraham was an idolater who lived in central Asia. He did not know God or his saving purposes. God revealed himself to Abraham and entered into a covenant relationship with him. This covenant was renewed with Abraham's son Isaac and his grandson Jacob, who was the father of the twelve tribes of Israel. This is why we refer to the Jews as God's "chosen people." In the covenant, however, repeated numerous times, God makes a three-fold promise to Abraham and his offspring. First, he promises to personally bless him with numerous descendants. He promises to multiply Israel and make them as numerous as the stars in the sky or the sand on the seashore. Second, he promises to bless Abraham's descendants and make them into a great nation. Finally, he promises that through Abraham and his offspring, he will bless every nation in the world. Eventually it becomes clear that this global blessing is made possible through one particular offspring of Abraham, namely, Jesus Christ.

Scripture Reading

Genesis 12:1–3

Genesis 17:1–8

Genesis 22:1–18

Genesis 26:3–5

Genesis 28:10–17

Deuteronomy 5:6–21

9

What was the purpose of the Law?

When God brought the people of Israel out of Egypt with "a mighty hand and an outstretched arm," that deliverance from slavery to freedom became a central orienting event in the minds and hearts of God's people. The Exodus was celebrated and remembered every year at Passover, and it became the focal point of their identity as a people. They were the people whom God had redeemed from slavery, who had experienced the mighty testimony of his judgments against their captors and his miracles of provision on their behalf, and who waited in hope for a Messiah who would bring an even greater deliverance, of which this one was just a forerunner.

God's purpose in delivering them was much greater than just delivering them "out" of something, namely oppression and slavery. His purpose was also to bring them "into" something—a life of holiness by which they would truly reflect his image in the world. In order to instruct and form this newly redeemed people into a faithful covenant people, God gave them the revelation of the Law at Mount Sinai. Through the Law, God was demonstrating his own holiness and covenantal love, and also revealing to the people of Israel how they were to live and act as his covenant people. You can think of the Law as providing a tangible picture, through words, of what life is meant to look like when lived in proper obedience to our loving heavenly Father.

There are 613 laws in the Old Testament. However, they are all expressions or further explanations of the Ten Commandments. Thus, the Ten Commandments are the great summary of God's Law. They show us how we are supposed to live, and give the broad parameters of a life which is faithful to God and our neighbor. If you look at the Ten Commandments, you will see that the first four commandments focus on our relationship with God. The last six focus on our relationship with our neighbor. You might say that the Ten Commandments represent the basic grammar or alphabet of the holy life. They are God's way of clearly setting forth the basic need for a human reorientation towards God and neighbor which sin has distorted. Sin turns us away from God and neighbor, whereas the Law reorients us back towards God and neighbor. This is why many centuries later Jesus said that the entire Law, including the 613 and the Ten Commandments could be summarized as simply, "to love the Lord your God with all your heart, soul, mind and strength and to love your neighbor as yourself."

Our inability to fulfill or live out the Law is a testimony to our need for salvation, which is why Paul declared in Galatians 3:24 that the Law was a "tutor to lead us to Christ" (NASB). Just as Moses led the people out of their captivity in Egypt and into the Promised Land where they lived under the covenant and Law of God, so Jesus has led us out of an even greater captivity (sin and death) and brought us to a lasting promised land (New Creation). Jesus is the fulfillment of not only the priesthood and the sacrificial system, but also of the Law itself. Thus, the deepest purpose of the Law is not only to show us the holiness of God, but to lead us to Christ.

Scripture Reading

Exodus 20:1–17	Romans 2:17–3:24
Deuteronomy 5:1–21	Galatians 3:6–25

10

What was the purpose of the priesthood and the sacrificial system?

God established a priesthood out of the tribe of Levi (one of the twelve tribes of Israel) in order to mediate the Law and forgiveness of God to the people of God. The priests served as a constant reminder of the gravity of sin, the need for redemption, and the power of declared forgiveness. The priests mediated the daily sacrifices and extended the word of forgiveness to the people.

Once a year the people of God would set apart a special day known as the Day of Atonement (Yom Kippur). This was the holiest day of the year. No one would work on that day and everyone would fast and confess their sins before God. The high priest would enter the holy of holies and offer a special sacrifice for the sins of the people, including the sins of the priests. The blood of a bull would be sprinkled on the altar as a sign of the payment for sins. One of the most notable features of the Day of Atonement was when the priest took two goats and brought them into the presence of God. One of the goats would be sacrificed for the sins of the people. The priest would then lay his hands on the second goat and confess the sins of Israel over the goat and then take the goat out into the wilderness and release it. It was symbolic of their sins being atoned for and carried far away from the people of God.

Sacrifices were an important part of the life of ancient Israel. There were burnt offerings, grain offerings, fellowship offerings, sin offerings, and guilt offerings, among others. The purpose of all these sacrifices was to underscore the need for atonement. God's holiness demands that sin be paid for. God's mercy and grace provided a way for sin to be atoned. God's holiness and mercy meet in the sacrificial system mediated by priests. However, it should be noted that the root meaning of the word "atonement" is to "cover up." In the sacrificial system the priests were authorized to declare people forgiven, but it was in anticipation of a greater sacrifice by a greater High Priest. The Old Testament could only temporarily "cover up" sins. It was like temporarily sweeping them under the rug. The blood of bulls and goats, declares the New Testament, could not really take sins away.

It was a temporary arrangement. The priests were themselves sinners so it had to be repeated year after year.

When Jesus Christ came, he offered a final and complete sacrifice of himself. He was the only true pure sacrifice. He was God's true High Priest, not just a temporary agent, and he was truly without sin. His sacrifice was once for all and final, and did not need to be repeated. He did not enter into a humanly constructed "holy of holies" but into the very presence of God in heaven. So, looking back we see that the entire priesthood and sacrificial system were but a shadow anticipating what was to come in a final and complete way in and through Jesus Christ. The human race was being prepared through priests and sacrifices to understand what would later take place through the incarnation, death, and resurrection of Jesus Christ.

Scripture Reading

Exodus 29:1-9
Leviticus 1:1–17, 5:14–6:7

Hebrews 4:14–5:10
Hebrews 7:11–8:2

11

What was the purpose of the temple?

In the Garden of Eden, God was fully present with Adam and Eve. The whole of creation was filled with the manifest presence of the glory of God. In a certain sense, the whole of creation was a temple for God's presence, with his rule and reign extending over all he had made. However, with the entrance of sin, humanity experienced for the first time the absence of God. Sin is, at its root, a broken relationship. To put it another way, whenever we sin we are choosing—at that point—the absence of God in our lives. Sin might be understood as all those places in our lives and in our actions where we have said "no" to God's presence and we have shut God out.

God's plan is to once again fill the world with his glory and presence. The temple (preceded by the tabernacle or "tent of meeting" in the wilderness), was the provision God made for this return of his presence among his people. It had an outer court, an inner holy place where sacrifices were offered, and an inner sanctuary known as the holy of holies where the high priest would enter once a year.

There was a heavy curtain which separated the holy of holies from the holy place, and no one except the high priest was allowed to enter. In the holy of holies was a special ornate box known as the Ark of the Covenant which contained, among other things, the original stone tablets upon which were written the Ten Commandments. The top of this chest was known as the mercy seat since it was here that the high priest put the blood of the sacrifice and the people's sins were forgiven. When the sins were declared forgiven, God's presence would be manifest in the holy of holies. The temple was the ongoing sign of the presence of God among his people, and provided the one place where God could be approached. Thus, the temple represented the presence of God and the absence of sin.

In the New Testament we learn not only that Jesus is the High Priest and the final sacrifice, as noted earlier, but we also learn that he is the true Temple of God. In Jesus, the presence of God and the absence of sin are truly and finally found. When Jesus died upon the cross, one of the often neglected details is that at the moment of his death the heavy curtain which separated the holy of holies from the holy place was torn in two from the top down. It was the symbolic demonstration that the presence of God was no longer limited to one place, but was now, in Christ, made available to the whole world.

Indeed, wherever two or more are gathered in his name, the presence of God is there! God is now present with his people wherever they gather in the world. As the church continues to grow and spread, the presence of God continues to invade the world, dispelling darkness and sin, and reestablishing God's rightful rule and reign.

Scripture Reading

1 Kings 6:1–22
Hebrews 9:1–10:22
Revelation 21:1–5

12

Why did God become a man in Jesus Christ?

Although the Triune God is from all eternity, the Scriptures teach that at a certain point in time the second person of the Trinity became a man known as Jesus Christ, or Jesus the Messiah. This is known as the incarnation, which simply means "in the flesh." We have already noted how the entire human race fell into sin because of Adam's disobedience. We have also pointed out how the priests, temple, and sacrificial system were not able to fully solve the problem of sin. The principal reason for this is that the entire human race is made up of sinners and there is no one in the human race without sin. As Augustine said, "We are sinners by birth and by choice."

How can the human race be rescued out of rebellion and avoid inevitable condemnation when everyone, without exception, is bound under sin? The only way is to bring *another* Adam into the world; someone who, like that first

Adam, was without sin and who could once again have the choice to obey or disobey, but this time get it right. In other words, there had to be a way to go back and rewrite that first chapter of the human story recorded in Genesis chapter three on the Fall of Man.

But how is that possible? God knows that the whole human race is ineligible, so it couldn't be an inside job. God devised a plan from the "outside" which involved the radical idea of God himself entering into human history. But even this was not without problems. He had to find a way to enter the human race in an abnormal way that would not pass on the sin nature, and yet would still be fully human. So Christ was born of a virgin into the human race as a second Adam.

Unless God himself entered into human history, there was no way we could escape the entangling web of sin and the resulting condemnation which comes through that sin. The incarnation is, therefore, the greatest testimony to God's desire to redeem the world and to make good on his promise to Abraham to bless all the nations of the world through his offspring.

Scripture Reading

Isaiah 9:6
Luke 1:26–35
John 1:14

Romans 5:12–20
Galatians 4:4

13

What was the purpose of Jesus' life and ministry?

The Gospels devote considerable time to telling us the story of the life of Jesus Christ. We find Jesus teaching the multitudes, training disciples, casting out demons, and proclaiming the in-breaking of the Kingdom of God. But if we step back and look at the whole life of Jesus, we should see it as Jesus rewriting the history of the human race. Jesus is showing us how God designed life to be before it was distorted by sin and rebellion against God. The Scriptures tell us that Satan tried desperately to tempt Jesus, but at every point of assault, Jesus, unlike Adam, chose to obey God, to reject the forces of the rebellion, and to live without sin.

If we trust in Jesus Christ, then we participate in his obedience in the same way that we participated in Adam's rebellion. When Jesus is tempted in the desert and declares that he will love the Lord God and serve him only, you are there with him in the desert learning how, in Christ, we can resist the devil and serve God. When Christ confronts the demonic world, exercising authority over the rebellion, you are there in Christ defeating the enemy. You are in Christ as he obeyed, just as you were once in Adam as he disobeyed! In every situation where the first Adam disobeyed, the second Adam obeyed. Whenever the first Adam said no to God, this Adam said yes. In Christ, the entire history of the human race is being rewritten, and now we *can* turn the clock back and get it right.

The final test culminates in the Garden of Gethsemane. The whole thing started in the Garden of Eden, and now here we are in another garden, facing the same question of obedience. The Second Adam is now poised to obey or disobey, just as the first Adam was in the first garden. After a whole lifetime of choosing the Father's will above his own, is Jesus prepared to choose God's will in this final test? Is he ready to take upon himself the sins of the whole world, to suffer separation from his Father, to bear the wrath of God for all the sins of humanity from Adam until the end of time? This is the most intense moment of human history; the decision of Jesus at this very moment, on his knees sweating blood and crying out to God, holds the whole fate of the human race in the balance. Finally, Jesus says the words which have changed the world: "Not *my* will, but thine be done."

At the heart of our rebellion against God is the declaration through thought and word we want *our* will to be done. However, in that moment, Jesus reverses the motto of the rebellion and declares that he wants to do God's will. This effectively turns the tables on all the powers of evil. Man's great "no" of rebellion is being swallowed up in Christ's great "yes" of obedience.

The whole of Jesus' life and ministry can, therefore, be summed up as the invasion of the Kingdom of God into this world. The Kingdom of God is the rule and reign of God. Apart from Christ the world is oriented towards the assertion of self and participation in the rebellion against God. That orientation leads only to death, as Adam was warned in Genesis 2:17. But in the life, teaching, and ministry of Jesus we see another path set forth which leads not to death, but to life.

Scripture Reading

John 10:7–11

John 18:37

Romans 5:15–19

1 Timothy 1:15–17

14

Why did Jesus Christ suffer and die upon the cross?

The cross has become the central symbol of the Christian faith. It is truly amazing that such a symbol of torture devised by the Roman Empire to inflict cruel punishment on common criminals would become the most recognizable symbol of love and grace in the world. However, for God's plan of redemption to be complete, it was not only necessary for Jesus to live and walk among us, but also that he die for the sins of the world. He had to become the perfect, sinless sacrifice which could atone for sins, once and for all.

To understand why his death on a *cross* was so important we must go all the way back to the dawn of creation when sin first entered the world. When Adam sinned, we immediately see three effects which rippled out from that first sin: fear, guilt, and shame. It is after the first sin that we discover that Adam was afraid, and filled with guilt and shame. He tried to hide from the presence of God because he felt shame and fear. It was, therefore, essential that the death of Jesus overturn every aspect of sin, including fear, guilt, and shame.

In the West we normally associate sin with guilt, so the mere fact of Jesus' death, regardless of how it occurred, would be sufficient to satisfy our guilt and make us right with God. From the standpoint of guilt, the death of Christ is like a legal transaction. We are guilty of innumerable sins. Jesus died for those sins, thereby making a full payment which atones for them. Therefore God, as judge, is able to maintain his holiness in forgiving us and declaring us "not guilty" through the atoning sacrifice of Christ.

Other cultures are governed not so much by guilt as by shame or fear. The public humiliation of Jesus which involved torture and a mock coronation with the crown of thorns and the royal robe is a crucial feature of the suffering of Jesus. It was essential that his death be a public act of shame and humiliation, especially one in which Jesus was shamed and mocked by his own people. In many parts of the world one's place within a larger social context is the primary source of one's identity. For Jesus to be reviled and ridiculed by his own people was a source of unbearable shame.

Furthermore, the cross was the most feared form of punishment in the world. The fact that Jesus faced this particular kind of death is also his way of bearing our greatest fears. Therefore, we should understand the death of Jesus not simply as being nailed to a cross to satisfy a judicial requirement of God. In addition, the entire passion of Christ from his arrest and imprisonment, to his arraignment, to his beating, to his lonely walk publicly carrying the cross, to his being stripped naked and nailed to the beam is all part of the great drama of redemption whereby Jesus Christ faced *all* the ravages of sin (guilt, shame, and fear) and triumphed over them through the cross.

Scripture Reading

Luke 23:23–35

John 19:18–20

Acts 4:8–12

1 Corinthians 1:18–25

1 Corinthians 2:2

1 Corinthians 15:3–4

Galatians 6:14–15

Colossians 2:13–15

Hebrews 2:5–18

Hebrews 10:19–22

15

Why did Jesus Christ rise from the dead and ascend into heaven?

If the cross is the central symbol of Christianity, then the resurrection is the central proclamation of the church. Paul says that if Christ has not been raised, we are still in our sins, our preaching is useless, and our hope is in vain. If you examine the sermons of the early church found in the book of Acts, they all focus on the power of the resurrection as the basis upon which the gospel can be rightly proclaimed to the world. There are three main reasons for this.

First, the bodily resurrection of Jesus is the vindication of God the Father that Jesus the Son was, indeed, victorious over sin, death, and hell. In Jesus Christ, the Fall has been overturned and a new and living Way has been opened up whereby all people are called to come and receive his forgiveness and be restored into a right relationship with God.

Second, the resurrection of Jesus is the guarantee of our own future bodily resurrections at the end of time. Despite all the popular songs and language to the contrary, Christianity does not believe that God is merely "saving souls." God has redeemed the entire person—body, soul, and spirit! Jesus' resurrection is seen by the early Christians as the firstfruits of the general resurrection of us all at the end of time. So, how do we know that God will raise us from the dead on the last day? Because it has already happened once to Jesus, so we know that the same God that raised Jesus from the dead is able to raise our mortal bodies.

Finally, the resurrection of Christ is what sets Christianity apart from all other religions in the world. Without the resurrection, Christianity begins to look a lot more like Islam or Judaism. The resurrection reminds us that Christianity is not merely about a new ethical teaching or some lofty ideas about how to live a more fulfilled life. Christianity is rooted in a specific historical act. God acted in history by sending Jesus into the world and then by raising him from the dead. Buddha is in the grave. Muhammad is in the grave. Confucius is in the grave. Jesus is the Risen and Living Lord!

The ascension of Christ is the completion of the earthly mission of Jesus. In the incarnation Jesus was sent to earth, he lived, died on the cross, and then he was raised to life on the third day. The ascension is the exaltation of Jesus back to the right hand of the Father in heaven.

When we think of Jesus today, we should think of him as reigning over his people. This does not mean simply that he is seated on a distant throne above the universe. Rather, it means that by his Spirit he is present and ruling wherever the church gathers in his name. Jesus is on the throne, but that throne is now present wherever his people are gathered and whenever the sacraments are given. He is no longer walking by the Sea of Galilee. He is no longer on the cross. He is waiting for all those who oppose his righteous rule to recognize his Lordship. He is interceding for us at the right hand of the Father, and he is reigning over us as the Lord of glory.

Scripture Reading

Matthew 28:1–10
Luke 24:50–53
Acts 2:22–41
Acts 4.32 35
Romans 1:1–5
Romans 6:1–11
1 Corinthians 15:12–20
Philippians 3:1–11

16

Who is the Holy Spirit and why was he sent?

As noted earlier, the Trinity is the way the church has come to best understand God's self-revelation of who he is. God is One. Yet, the one God has revealed himself as Father, Son, and Holy Spirit. The Holy Spirit is a full and eternal person of the Trinity, fully co-equal with the Father and the Son. A church which only focuses on Jesus Christ will not, in the long run, be a healthy, mature church. When we think of the Holy Spirit we should see him fulfilling three major roles in the work of salvation.

First, the Holy Spirit is the empowering presence of the living God. The Holy Spirit is not an impersonal force. The Holy Spirit is God himself acting in his world and in our lives. He draws us by his grace to the Father. He intercedes with us and within us, helping us to pray. The Holy Spirit teaches and admonishes us when we read Scripture. He applies and nurtures the fruit of the Spirit in our lives (love, joy, peace, patience, goodness, kindness, gentleness, faithfulness, and self-control). The Holy Spirit assures us of our forgiveness and our adoption as the children of God. In short, the Holy Spirit mediates the presence of God in our lives and in the church.

Second, the Holy Spirit empowers the church for effective service, witness, and global mission. Just before Jesus ascended into heaven, he promised to send us the Holy Spirit who would empower us to be his witnesses to the ends of the earth (Acts 1:8). It is the Holy Spirit who enables the church to serve sacrificially and to be an effective witness unto Christ and the gospel. There are thousands of people-groups who still have not received the good news about Jesus Christ. It is the Holy Spirit who makes sure that the gospel is proclaimed to the ends of the earth through the empowered witness of the church.

Finally, the Holy Spirit is the One who continues to manifest redemptive signs of God's kingdom breaking into the world. The good news of God's powerful work in this world did not stop at the cross and resurrection of Jesus Christ. It is too small to think that we are called to simply proclaim something that happened in history thousands of years ago While the cross and resurrection form the central proclamation of the church, we also acknowledge that the good news of God's reign continues to unfold. All the future realities of heaven (healing, forgiveness, reconciliation, deliverance from evil, etc.) continue to break into the world through the presence of the Holy Spirit. Men and women are healed by the power of the Holy Spirit. They experience forgiveness and reconciliation with one another. The poor and downcast receive hope. The Holy Spirit applies all the future realities of the New Creation into the present. This process will not be fully complete until Jesus returns, but if we look around we can see that God is still at work by his Spirit, reconciling the world to himself.

Scripture Reading

Genesis 1:1–2

Joel 2:28–32

Mark 1:8

Luke 24:45–49

John 3:5–8

John 6:44

John 14:15–26

John 16:5–16

Acts 1:8

Acts 2:1–13

Acts 4:29–31

Acts 5:3–4

Acts 13:2

Romans 8:26

Ephesians 4:30

17

What is prevenient (preceding) grace?

Earlier we learned that part of God's nature is the desire to reveal himself to us. God is not merely interested in giving us rules to live by. He wants us to *know* him and enter into a covenant relationship with him through Jesus Christ. This self-revealing nature of God comes out in many ways, including in creation, in our consciences, in Scripture, and ultimately in Jesus Christ.

It is important to understand that salvation never begins with anything we do, but always as a response to something God has done. To think that salvation begins with our repenting of our sins and asking Jesus into our hearts is not the way the Scriptures reveal the whole process of salvation. Rather, salvation always begins with God's prior action. He acts, and we accept or resist. It always happens in that pattern.

One way of talking about all the ways God prepares us to receive the gospel is to use the term, "prevenient (or preceeding) grace." Prevenient grace refers to all those acts of grace in our lives prior to our becoming a Christian. We know that such grace exists because Jesus said that "no one can come to me unless the Father who sent me draws him" (John 6:44). There is a "drawing" or "preparing" which precedes our actual conversion.

The other reason we know that God's grace must precede our decision to follow Christ is that the Scriptures teach us that we are dead in our trespasses and sins apart from Christ (Eph. 2:1). The Scriptures do not teach that we are merely sick or that our overall spiritual progress is slow, but that we are spiritually dead. (This is another great distinctive feature of Christianity.) This means that we are incapable of helping ourselves or saving ourselves without God's prior action.

Most Christians believe in the doctrine of total depravity. That means that humans are dead in their sins and cannot do anything to help or improve their spiritual state before God. However, it is also a Christian position to believe in free will. This means that we affirm that God wants us to act and make decisions for him. The problem is this: How can a spiritually dead person act or decide to give their lives to

Christ? The Bible is full of injunctions to act—people are *called* to repent, to believe, to come, to decide, and so forth. The answer is the doctrine of prevenient grace. This is the bridge between human depravity and the free exercise of human will. Prevenient grace is a sovereign act of God whereby he lifts the human race out of its depravity and grants us the capacity to respond further to God's grace. It is God's act of unmerited favor. It is God's light "which enlightens everyone" (John 1:9 ESV), which lifts us up and allows us to exercise our will and respond to the grace of Christ.

God takes the initiative to create a universal capacity for the human race to receive his grace. Many, of course, still resist his will and persist in rebellion against God. The doctrine of prevenient grace protects the church from views which argue that there is no sin nature. It also protects the church from views which argue that Jesus only died for those who have been elected before all creation to be followers of Christ. Prevenient grace preserves both the depravity of the human race and our confidence that Jesus died for every person who has ever lived or will live. In fact, prevenient grace does not technically affirm free will in the sense that anyone can decide to follow Christ whenever they want, because this pushes salvation too much towards the idea that salvation depends on our initiative. Rather, what is sometimes called "free will" is actually "freed will," a will in bondage which has been set free by an unmerited act of God's grace. It is, of course, not free in every possible respect, since we are all still influenced by the effects of the Fall in many ways; but we now have a restored capacity which has enabled our heart, mind, and will to respond to God's grace.

Scripture Reading

Isaiah 55:1

John 1:9

John 6:44

John 12:32

John 16:8–11

Acts 14:17

Acts 16:13–15

Romans 2:4

1 Timothy 2:4–6

Titus 2:11

18

What is justification?

One of the most frequently misunderstood words in the church today is the word "salvation." The problem seems to be rooted in the broad ways that the Scripture itself uses the word. It may surprise you, but the New Testament refers to salvation as a past act, a present act, and a future act. For example, there are passages of Scripture which affirm that we "have been" saved, we "are being" saved, and we "shall be" saved. According to the New Testament, all of these are true.

One way to understand this is to picture salvation as a stool which is held up by three legs. Salvation is the overarching concept and can, at times, be used for the three more precise terms for each of the legs of the stool. The first leg is *justification*, which primarily refers to a past action. The second leg is *sanctification*, primarily referring to a current operation of God in the life of the believer. The third leg is *glorification*, which primarily refers to a future state of the believer once we are finally in the full presence of God.

So, this study does not actually merely ask the big question: What is salvation? Instead, we ask the more precise questions: What is justification? What is sanctification? What is glorification? Once you understand those terms, then the meaning of salvation will be made clear, because it is nothing more than the sum of those three questions.

Justification refers to an act of God whereby he declares sinners forgiven for their sins and made right before him. The Scriptures do not give us a single metaphor or picture of how we are to understand the death of Christ. Instead, several metaphors are given, all of which convey different facets of the full meaning of Christ's death.

The first idea is that the death of Jesus was a sacrifice, rendering what we call a "substitutionary atonement." This means that Christ died in our place and bore our sins upon himself. It draws upon the Old Testament idea whereby the lifeblood of a lamb or bull was sacrificed in the place of the sinner. The sins were transferred from the sinner to the sacrificial animal. We already noted that it was actually impossible for the blood of a lamb or bull to truly take away sins. Jesus became the final substitution for our sins, fulfilling all those sacrifices which were offered in faith over the centuries. When someone asks how an Old Testament believer was justified, we can say with assurance that they were justified in precisely the same way we are—namely, through the death of Jesus Christ. The difference is that they looked forward in anticipation of the true substitution, whereas we look back in remembrance of that true substitution.

The second idea is that of redemption. In the ancient world a slave could be purchased out of slavery by making a payment. This payment "redeemed" the slave and purchased his freedom. The New Testament pictures us as slaves to sin and in bondage to Satan. On the cross, Jesus pays the debt, purchases our redemption, and sets us free from our bondage to sin. He redeems his enslaved people.

The third idea is a picture of a courtroom and a judicial process. In this picture we have symbolically been brought before the Judge, our sins have been exposed, and we have been declared guilty before God and sentenced to death. It is a righteous and just verdict. However, before we are removed from the courtroom, the Judge announces that he is prepared to satisfy the demands of justice by dying on behalf of the sins of the guilty party. In this picture, Jesus takes on the "curse of the Law" by accepting the just penalty for our sins upon himself, and we are actually declared "not guilty!" Christ thereby simultaneously satisfies the necessary demand for justice, and extends mercy and grace to the condemned person.

The fourth idea is that of a great cosmic battle, out of which Jesus Christ emerges as the triumphant victor. In this metaphor all the powers of evil, death, and darkness are arrayed against Jesus and the people of God. Since Jesus is our champion, the death of Jesus Christ is first perceived to be the final defeat of our hope. Instead, through the resurrection the tables are turned, and what appeared to be the defeat of Jesus turns out, in fact, to be the defeat of Satan and the overturning of death. Christ is our victor. He has defeated sin and death, triumphing over them and vanquishing all our enemies.

A fifth picture of justification is that of reconciliation, whereby the broken relationship between God and humanity is restored through the mediating priesthood of Jesus Christ. He is simultaneously both priest and sacrifice, bridging the broken gap between God and humanity, and restoring the fellowship which had been broken by sin.

There are several other metaphors in the New Testament, but these are some of the central ones. Collectively they help us to capture a glimpse of how a condemned sinner can be declared righteous before God. All of these metaphors are pointing to various facets of what it means to be justified before God.

Scripture Reading

Isaiah 55:6–7
Joel 2:12–13
Acts 11:14
Acts 16:25–34
Romans 3:21–28
Romans 4:1–16
Romans 5:1–11

Romans 10:5–17
2 Corinthians 5:17–21
Galatians 2:15–16
Ephesians 2:1–10
Colossians 1:20
Colossians 2:13–15
Titus 3:4–7

19

What is sanctification?

While justification is that doctrine which makes us think of all the ways in which Jesus Christ's death and resurrection reconciled us to God, sanctification is the doctrine which reminds us that salvation is the work of the Triune God. Sanctification means to be "made holy," and is one of the primary functions of the Holy Spirit in our lives. Once justified, God declares us righteous, but it is what Martin Luther, the great sixteenth century reformer of the church, said was an "alien righteousness." In other words, we are not truly righteous, we are merely *declared* righteous because of the righteousness of another.

However, God is not merely interested in us being forgiven with an alien righteousness. He wants to see us actually transformed into the likeness of Jesus Christ. This is primarily the work of the Holy Spirit. His work is to bring all the fruit of the Holy Spirit into our lives, including love, joy, patience, kindness, goodness, gentleness, faithfulness, and self-control. Sanctification is not just about what we *avoid*, but what we *produce*—fruitfulness. In the gospel, faith and fruit must meet and be joyfully wed.

Christians have different views as to how this process takes place. For some it is an incremental, day-by-day process which continues throughout our lifetime, never reaching completion until we finally meet Christ through death or his return, and we are then brought fully into conformity with his righteousness as we are removed from the very presence of sin. Other Christians, particularly those in the Wesleyan tradition, believe that sanctification is not merely a process, but also involves a specific event in the presence of the Holy Spirit in the same way that our justification involves a specific event in the presence of Jesus Christ. This event has many different names, including being "baptized in the Holy Spirit" or receiving a "second blessing" or being made "perfect in love" or "entire sanctification."

It is important to point out that the idea of an experience like this with the Holy Spirit has often been misunderstood. It is misunderstood primarily because when we hear the word "sanctification," we often think of it as a forensic term (i.e., being sanctified means that you are divinely certified before God's court of justice as someone without any sin in your life and, once sanctified, you will never sin again). That is not what the Scriptures teach concerning sanctification.

For Wesley, sanctification is not really a legal or forensic term at all. You could be justified alone on a deserted island, but sanctification is inherently relational. In fact, it is relational to the core. It is what happens when we are brought back fully into relationship with the Triune God.

As we noted earlier, when we sin, in that moment of choosing sin, we are actually electing the absence of God in our lives at that point. Sanctification is what fully restores our relationship with God, not merely by justifying us, but by turning our hearts back towards God. Sanctification means that your whole life—your body and your spirit—have been reoriented. Entire sanctification means that our entire heart has been reoriented towards the joyful company of the Triune God. It is not merely a long road whereby we march out, step by step, from a long road of sin. It is our joyful union with the Triune God, wherein we actually desire and pursue holiness in our lives.

Holiness is the crown of true happiness. Sanctification is what turns our hearts to long for that holiness, to seek and pursue it, and to be purified from everything that "contaminates body and spirit, perfecting holiness out of reverence for God" (2 Cor. 7:1).

True righteousness is not merely God looking at us with a different set of glasses. *Alien* righteousness must become *native* righteousness, *imputed* righteousness must become *actualized* righteousness, *declared* righteousness must become *embodied* righteousness—wrought in us not by our own strength, but through the power of the living God. We are marked, oriented, and reoriented by love.

Sin is still encamped around us on every side, but it is no longer our ally. We burn the secret agreements we have—to nod and wink at sin in the night while we confess Christ in the day. We leave behind the agonizingly torn hearts, where we live under condemnation because sin is always creeping back into our lives. To be sanctified is to receive a second blessing—a great gift from God—a gift which changes your heart, re-orients your relationships with the Triune God and with others, giving you the capacity to love God and your neighbor in new and profound ways. It transforms your perspective—because your heart is re-oriented. Sanctified people still sin. However, the difference is that in the life of a sanctified person, sin is a permanent enemy and no longer a secret lover!

The language of "entire sanctification" uses the word "entire" in reference to Greek, not Latin. In Greek, "entire" or "complete" can still be improved upon. It is simply a new orientation which no longer looks back towards the old life, but rather looks forward longingly to the New Creation. It is a life which has been engulfed by new realities, not the realities of that which is passing away. A sanctified person is caught up into a higher frame of reference in which the heart has been reoriented. It is what Wesley once called a "self-forgetful heart," and a life engulfed by "perfect love."

One of the best stories I ever heard for "perfect love" was a story told by Robert Coleman, who taught at Asbury for twenty-seven years. Robert was working in the garden on a hot day, and sweat was pouring off his body. His son saw him through the window of the house working so hard, and decided to bring him a glass of water. He went down to the kitchen, pulled up a stool, and managed to reach up to the sink. He picked up a dirty glass laying in the sink, filled it with lukewarm water, and brought it out to his dad. Robert commented, "The glass may have been dirty and the water warm, but it was brought to me in perfect love."

Scripture Reading

Leviticus 11:44–45
Matthew 5:48
John 17:13–19
Acts 20:32
Acts 26:15–18
Romans 13:11–14
Romans 15:14–16
1 Corinthians 6:11
2 Corinthians 1:21–22

2 Corinthians 7:1
Galatians 5:24
Ephesians 1:13–14
Ephesians 4:1–3
Colossians 3:12–14
1 Thessalonians 5:23
2 Thessalonians 2:13
Hebrews 6:1

20

What is glorification?

Glorification refers to the final state of believers after Christ returns. Our bodies will be physically resurrected and we will receive a resurrection body which is, mysteriously, both spiritual and physical (see meditation for Day Twenty-Eight). Before justification we were in bondage to sin. After justification we are freed from the *penalty* of sin. Through sanctification we are freed from the *power* of sin. At glorification we are delivered from the very *presence* of sin. In this glorified state we are able to experience the fullness of the original purpose of our creation.

This final state is known as the "New Creation," since the Scriptures tell us that God creates a new heaven and a new earth. In the New Creation we will be engaged in all the kinds of industrious work and projects and inventions and building that we are involved with here, *but without the presence of sin*.

Indeed, this is the great transforming fact about the New Creation. It is not a spirit-type existence where we sit endlessly on a cloud with the wings of an angel, as we see in medieval artwork. We will not be standing forever in a worship service that never has a benediction. Rather, we should see that all of life becomes an act of worship, and the absence of sin completely transforms the very nature of life and work.

In the Garden of Eden, before the Fall of Man, we were commanded to work. Work is not a result of life in a sinful world. What changed after the Fall is that work became toilsome and wearying and fraught with sin. In the New Creation, we will be unleashed into endless creativity and deeper discoveries about God's creation. Our work will be filled with joyful productivity and will be free from drudgery. For all eternity we will be brought deeper and deeper into the full glory and mystery of the Triune God. We will learn to love him and one another in deeper and deeper ways.

We will, ultimately, be like him because we will finally see him face-to-face. As John says, "Beloved, we are God's children now, and what we will be has not yet appeared; but we know that when he appears we shall be like him, because we shall see him as he is" (1 John 3:2 ESV). When John says we shall be "like him" it does not mean that we will have taken on the nature of God himself. We will always be created beings, totally dependent upon his life for our existence. But we will be "like him" in the sense that we share more and more in his holiness, purity, and joy.

Scripture Reading

John 17:22–24
Romans 8:29–30
1 Corinthians 15:35–44
2 Corinthians 4:16–17

Colossians 3:4
2 Timothy 2:9–13
1 John 3:1–3

21

What is the church?

The church is the joyful company of all those who have been redeemed and brought into right relationship with God. Jesus declared that he was going to build a new community known as the church. Jesus did not use the more common expression of a "congregation" or a "synagogue" to describe his new community, but the word "church." The word in the Greek is the word for being called to a public assembly. It simultaneously reminds us that we have been called out of a life of sin into a new community, and also that this community is a public assembly designed for men, women, and children alike who have been baptized and brought into this new redeemed life. It is not, like the earlier word, limited to Jews, but is now open to the whole human race, Jew and Gentile. It is a community of prayer, of teaching, of training, of discipline, and it is the place where we dwell in the presence of God and commune with him at the Lord's Supper or Eucharist. We are not merely saved as individuals but we are saved as a *people*.

As explored earlier, precisely because sin is fundamentally a broken relationship, it is important that we are brought into new, redeemed relationships so that we can demonstrate to the world what it means to be made right before God. The church is designed to be a little outpost of heaven in the midst of a lost world.

Another phrase used to describe the church is the "Body of Christ." This expression emphasizes the organic nature of the gathered people of God. The church is not the building where we meet for worship and prayer. The church is the gathering of God's people, each discovering their gifts and the ways we together manifest the presence of Christ in the world. Paul's description of the "body" reminds us that we each have a purpose in the functioning of the whole, and we each have gifts which work together in service to one another and the world. It is in the church that we discover the community God intended for us, and are empowered for the global mission of the gospel to all peoples and to every corner of the earth.

What is the relationship between the church and the Kingdom of God? The Kingdom of God refers to the reign and rule of God. It is the Kingdom which is breaking into the world and which gives birth to the church. The church is the living witness of the rule and reign of God. In the church we are to see manifest in dozens of ways how God's rule and reign impact daily life, families, society, and the world. In other words, the church is designed to be the tangible expression of the rule and reign of God.

Scripture Reading

Matthew 16:13–19
Acts 9:31
Romans 12:4–8

1 Corinthians 12:12–31
Ephesians 2:19–20
Hebrews 12:22–23

22

What is the Bible and why was it given to the church?

The Bible is the record of God's self-revelation to his people. In the Scriptures we discover the specifics of who God is, what God is like, what his plan is, how to receive forgiveness, what it means to live a holy life, our responsibility for those who are suffering, and our obligations to a lost world. The Bible is the standard by which all true Christian belief and practice must be judged and evaluated. However, the Bible was not designed to be merely a rule book or a how-to manual. Rather, the Bible gives us God's self-revelation in the midst of specific situations and contexts, whether in the life of Israel or the challenges of first-century churches.

As we read the Bible, we begin to capture a glimpse of God's majestic plan. Since God's character and ways do not change, we are able to see more of who he is. We capture glimpses of his holiness and his majestic purity and righteousness. In fact, whenever we sit down to read the Bible or hear someone reading Scripture in a public service, we should always picture ourselves as reading the Bible in the presence of the Risen Christ. We should never read the Bible in isolation from the presence of the Triune God. The Holy Spirit is present teaching us and applying the work of Christ to our lives. As we read we are brought into the presence of Christ himself in new and remarkable ways.

God declares that the Bible is "God-breathed." This is much more than the word "inspiration" normally conveys to the human mind. When we think of "inspiration" we think of Bach writing a beautiful musical composition or a painter who is "inspired" to paint a beautiful painting or an architect who is "inspired" to create an amazing new design. The Bible rises above this use of the word "inspiration." In fact, the phrase "God-breathed" implies more of an ex-spiration than an in-spiration—the Scriptures are the very words of God breathed out of his mouth.

This does not violate the idea that Moses or the apostle Paul or Peter or others actually wrote the words which are now conveyed to us in the Bible. Rather, it means that as they wrote, the Holy Spirit was with them and he restrained them from any errors so that what they actually wrote represented the very words of God himself. This is why we can, on the one hand, speak of Paul's style or choice of words, and yet, on the other hand, declare that the end result is the very words of God. Scripture represents a beautiful cooperation between God and man.

In fact, the Scriptures themselves reflect the incarnation. Jesus was fully God, yet fully man. He was a man in every sense of the word, fully human except for the presence of sin. Yet, in the mystery of the incarnation, all of the fullness of God was also present in Jesus Christ (Col. 2:9). In the same way, the Scriptures truly represent the words of real men writing in real situations. It is the word of man. Yet, because God restrained the writers from error and guided them in their choice of words, the result is the very words of God, breathed forth to the people of God.

Sometimes people speak of several words which together describe the sources of authority in the church—namely, Scripture, experience, reason, and tradition. It is certainly true that our own personal experience with God is very important, that we are called to bring our mind and reason to the reading of Scripture, and that we should listen to the voice of the church through the ages. However, these are not four equal sources of authority. Rather, we should understand that the Bible is the sole source of authority in the life of the church, and the other three should be seen as guides which help us in our understanding and interpretation of Scripture. Our experience, human reasoning, and even church tradition will fail us from time to time. However, Scripture alone is without error and is the only infallible guide to the church's faith and practice. Whenever the people of God lose their confidence in the Scriptures, the church suffers and the gospel becomes obscured by other agendas. The Bible, as the Word of God, must always be honored by the church of Jesus Christ if we are to be faithful to Christ.

Scripture Reading

Psalms 19:7–11
Psalms 119:89
Proverbs 30:5–6
Jeremiah 23:29
Jeremiah 30:1–2
Habakkuk 2:2

Matthew 4:4
John 10:35
1 Thessalonians 2:13
2 Timothy 3:16–17
Hebrews 4:12
2 Peter 1:20–21

23

What is a sacrament and how many are there?

When a person has been released from prison or rescued from some dire condition, the first thing they need is to receive a nice warm bath and a meal. These are universal symbols of grace and hospitality. To receive someone into your home and offer them a bath and a meal is one of the surest signs of full acceptance and a real relationship. This is, essentially, what God does with us after we are rescued from the bondage of sin, brought out of our imprisonment to Satan and into a new life in Christ.

Our first act is to receive baptism which is the Christian way of giving a new believer a "spiritual bath." This act simultaneously symbolizes both our cleansing from sin as well as a tangible reenactment of a death and resurrection. As we symbolically reenact Christ's own death and resurrection, we "die" to our sins and are raised to new life with Christ.

Likewise, Communion or the Lord's Supper is the place where we sit down at a table in the presence of Jesus Christ who serves as host, and we enjoy a meal together. In the early church the Lord's Supper was not merely the tiny tokens of bread and wine that we have today. Rather, it was a full meal, known as the love feast, which culminated in the symbolic eating of his body and drinking of his blood as a way of declaring that we are united with Christ in his death and resurrection. Today, communion has been separated from the larger meal so we may not fully recognize it as a "meal" with Jesus Christ, who spiritually stands at the head of the table as the host.

Jesus instituted these two ongoing practices in the church as a way of marking out the new life in Jesus Christ: baptism and the Lord's Supper. These two practices are normally known as sacraments. Some Christian traditions do not like the word "sacrament," but prefer the word "ordinance." A sacrament has been defined as "an outward and visible sign of an inward and spiritual grace." This means that it is an act of grace whereby God is truly present at the waters of baptism and at the table, and *he acts* in the lives of those who come to the waters of baptism and to the Lord's Supper. An ordinance, in contrast, emphasizes the action of the church in remembering. An ordinance is more of a regular reminder of what Christ did long ago, rather than an action of his real presence right now in the life of the believer.

You will likely recall the phrase from Jesus at the Last Supper, "This is my body; do this in remembrance of me." Some traditions emphasize the first part of the phrase, "this is my body," and call attention to the divine presence. Others draw attention to the second part of the phrase, "do this in remembrance of me," and focus upon looking back and remembering. Since all Christians believe in the general presence of God with all believers, those who emphasize the special presence of Jesus at the Lord's Supper often use the expression "real presence."

Two of the most common expressions for this sacred meal are "Communion" and "Lord's Supper," both of which are found in the writings of the apostle Paul to refer to this sacrament. In 1 Corinthians 10:16, he refers to our sharing in the body and blood of Christ. The word for sharing is literally *"communion* in the blood of Christ" and *"communion* in the body of Christ." The second term, "Lord's Supper," is used by Paul in 1 Corinthians 11:20 to describe the sacrament. A third term which is sometimes used for the meal is "Eucharist." This is a word which simply means "thanksgiving." In 1 Corinthians 11:24, the apostle Paul records that just prior to Jesus breaking the bread and giving the cup, he "gave thanks." Over time the church developed more formal, liturgical prayers which "gave thanks" prior to the breaking of the bread and the giving of the cup, known as the Great Thanksgiving. This was for the purpose of keeping the meal sacred, which is the larger context of why an extended discussion on the sacrament appears in Paul's letter to the church at Corinth. A new believer should recognize that all three terms, *Communion, Lord's Supper*, and *Eucharist*, are interchangeable terms for the same sacrament, and I would recommend that all three terms be embraced.

As for the terms "sacrament" and "ordinance," I think it is entirely appropriate to use the word "sacrament" and to understand both baptism and the Lord's Supper as ongoing means of grace in our lives. They are expressions of God's hospitality whereby we are renewed in our fellowship with him, experience his presence, receive his word of forgiveness and grace, and are empowered to go out into the world as his ambassadors.

Scripture Reading

Matthew 26:26–28

Matthew 28:19

Mark 14:22–24

Luke 22:19–20

Acts 2:38–39

Acts 16:14–15

Acts 16:31–33

Acts 18:8

Romans 6:3–5

1 Corinthians 10:16

1 Corinthians 11:23–29

Galatians 3:27–28

24

What are the "means of grace"?

The two sacraments, baptism and Lord's Supper, are not the only ways in which God extends grace to his people. The phrase "means of grace" is a broader category referring to all the ways God has appointed to convey his grace to men and women. The two sacraments are the best examples, and are called "sacraments" because Jesus himself instituted them and commanded us to observe them. Sacraments involve something physical like bread or water and are to be celebrated in community.

However, God is not limited to conveying grace only when we are gathered together as the church. God also conveys grace to us as individuals. Examples of this would include the reading of Scripture, hearing God's Word preached, prayer, fasting, serving the poor, and so forth. Broadly speaking, a means of grace refers to all the ways by which Christians grow stronger in their faith and grow in the grace of Christ.

In other words, they are God's instruments to convey grace, including prevenient grace, justifying grace, sanctifying grace and, ultimately, glorifying grace.

An unbeliever might be sitting next to a Christian on an airplane and the Christian may, in the course of their travels, share the gospel with this person. In the hearing of God's Word, the Holy Spirit acts to convict the person of their sin and they trust Jesus Christ for their salvation. In this instance, the sharing of God's Word on the airplane becomes a means of grace to the unbeliever. Likewise, if a Christian is going through a difficult time and is feeling absent from the presence of Christ, they may begin to sing or pray, and in that prayer they gain a renewed sense of the presence of Christ and a clearer direction as to how they should respond to the situation. This is another example of how prayer can become a "means of grace."

Of course, the Bible in and of itself, or a prayer in and of itself, has no power to change us. If we believed that, we would be affirming a form of magic. Rather, whenever we refer to a "means of grace" we acknowledge ultimately that only God is the true giver of grace, through the presence of Christ and the Holy Spirit. The term "means" simply reminds us that God uses ordinary things like words and prayers and actions to convey his presence to us, and whenever his presence is truly encountered (even if we don't feel it), then grace is conveyed. It is another way of saying that the church is not autonomous. The church does not "do good works" in the same way as one of the well-known, and worthy, organizations such as the Lion's Club or the Kiwanis Club. Instead, the church acts or speaks or prays in concert with Christ, and these actions or words all become channels or means through which God does his work. It is another example of the cooperation which God is building in his Kingdom. It is not enough for us to just sit back and wait for God to act. Instead, we roll up our sleeves and begin to serve the poor. We make a decision to get down on our knees and pray about something. We decide to put aside our fears and we share the gospel with someone. And, in the process, God comes alongside of us and uses these humble acts for his glory.

Scripture Reading

2 Kings 19:14–19

Nehemiah 8:1–10

Nehemiah 9:1

Jeremiah 36:4–8

Daniel 9:1–13

Matthew 6:5–18

Acts 6:1–4

Acts 13:1–3

Acts 14:23

25

What is the role of prayer in the life of the Christian?

Prayer is one of the means of grace previously noted. Prayer encompasses all the ways the believer—individually and as part of the assembled church—speaks to God, including petition, praise, lament, intercession, and so forth. Since prayer is such a central part of Christian life and faith, a number of special questions arise related to prayer which deserve special attention. For instance, if God is all-powerful, all-knowing, and all-good (essential attributes of God), then why does he not simply act on behalf of the lost or needy without the role of prayer? More to the point, why do we ask for things or tell God about things which he, quite obviously, already knows because he is God? If we need direction or healing or help or salvation, why does God not simply grant it for ourselves or others? If God has the power to help someone and does not do it, is he, therefore, culpable for the suffering or lostness or confusion which results because God failed to act? All of these questions, and many more, intersect at the point of prayer. Put simply, why do we pray and what role does prayer play in the larger work of God in the world?

Fundamental to our understanding of creation is that God did not desire to merely create an army of living machines who simply obey him and do his will. Throughout this study we have seen how God desires to include us in his work and, amazingly, to make us full participants in the unfolding of his salvation to the world. We have seen how Scripture itself comes to us in a collaborative way. We have ample testimony all around us which demonstrates how God uses people to preach the gospel, to administer the sacraments, to care for the environment, and to serve the poor, to name but a few. All of these things could be done by God directly, and with more efficiency, if he were to simply act autonomously. There is no outcome which is not attainable through the exercise of his sovereign power and dominion. Every broken heart could be healed, every toxic river could be cleansed, every rebellious heart could be turned, and every diseased body could be healed—all by his spoken word.

However, we have also seen that God's plan is much bigger than simply the meeting of certain final outcomes or objectives.

God is not interested in merely reaching a final outcome; rather, he works throughout the whole process of how we get there. He has determined that there is greater glory by working in us and through us and, indeed, in making us fellow participants in his redemptive work. Earlier we noted that no proper Christian action begins with us. We are always responding to God's prior initiative. This is true even of prayer. It is only because God has revealed his desire for justice that we pray for justice. It is only because God has already revealed his heart for the lost that we pray for the lost, and so forth. So, rather than seeing prayer as a human initiative which is trying to get an otherwise passive God to act in some way, we should see prayer as the means through which our own lives and wills are brought into concert with his divine will. We have the amazing privilege of witnessing God changing situations or people's hearts in response to prayer. Prayer really does change the course of the world. As Alfred Lord Tennyson once commented, "more things are wrought by prayer than this world ever dreamed of!" God has chosen to act in certain situations in direct response to the prayers of his people.

It is important to note, however, that God does not only call us to the life of prayer to participate in his work and to witness real transformations such as the healing of bodies, the reconciling of relationships, the salvation of the lost, and so forth. He also calls us to pray so that we, too, can be changed and so that our hearts may become more aligned with his heart. As we pray for the lost we begin to share in God's burden for the lost which was so great that he sent his only Son to die on a cross. As we pray for the needs of a poor family in our neighborhood, we begin to take their burdens into our own hearts and respond to their needs with the compassion of Christ which has been formed within us. So, prayer is not just for the outcome of changing this or that situation (though it is never less than that), but it is also part of God's work in changing us. We participate in his redemptive work by acting as his ambassadors in the world. We become participators in the extension of his grace and his mercy. All of this and more is wrought through prayer.

What may seem like unanswered prayer is often nothing more than God, in his wisdom, granting the time for other deeper realities to be worked in us and in the person for whom we are praying. It is also true that sometimes we pray for the wrong things because our own perspective is warped in some way. A wise person once said that when we conclude our prayer with the phrase, "In Jesus' Name," we are giving God editing rights on our prayers. Sometimes we pray for certain perceived outcomes which we believe would be right, good, or desirable, but God knows that our deepest need may be, in fact, precisely the opposite of our verbalized prayer. Finally, it is important to remember that some prayers are only fully answered in the resurrection at the end of time, when God will make all things right and wipe every tear away from our eyes.

Scripture Reading

I Kings 8:22–54	Psalms 88:2	Acts 6:4
Psalms 4:1	Psalms 88:13	Ephesians 1:16
Psalms 6:9	Psalms 102:1	Ephesians 6:18
Psalms 17:1	Psalms 102:17	Philippians 1:3–4
Psalms 32:6	Psalms 141:2	Philippians 1:19
Psalms 39:12	Psalms 143:1	Philippians 4:6
Psalms 42:8	Proverbs 15:29	Colossians 4:2
Psalms 54:2	Jonah 2:1–9	1 Thessalonians 1:2
Psalms 55:1	Matthew 21:22	1 Timothy 2:1
Psalms 61:1	Mark 11:24	Philemon 1:4
Psalms 65:2	Luke 6:12	Hebrews 5:7
Psalms 66:19–20	John 17:1–26	James 5:15–16
Psalms 69:13	Acts 1:14	Revelation 8:4
Psalms 84:8	Acts 2:42	
Psalms 86:6	Acts 3:1	

26

What is the gospel?

There is no more popular single word which summarizes the Christian faith than the word "gospel." It comes from a word in the New Testament which means "the good message" or "the good news." We often refer to the first four books of the New Testament as "the Gospels," meaning the books which contain the message of this good news. The apostle Paul, however, used the word "gospel" in the way we are asking this question when he reminded the church in Corinth "of the gospel I preached to you" (1 Cor. 15:1). He then went on to outline the key features of the good news which Christians preach. Paul said, "For I delivered to you as of first importance what I also received: that Christ died for our sins in accordance with the Scriptures, that he was buried, and that he was raised on the third day in accordance with the Scriptures." This demonstrates that while the good news of salvation is a very big concept, involving the work of the Triune God, the heart of the gospel is centered on the person and work of Jesus Christ.

This is not to diminish the good news of prevenient grace, for example, without which we could never respond to Christ. Nor does it diminish the good news of the Spirit's work to sanctify us. However, the point is that the good news finds its central focus in the work of Jesus Christ. This is the proclamation which transforms the world and gives the greatest insight into God's nature and character.

Scripture Reading

Matthew 24:14	Acts 14:21
Mark 1:15	Romans 1:15–17
Luke 9:6	1 Corinthians 15:1–5
Acts 8:25	Galatians 1:8–9
Acts 14:7	Colossians 1:21–23

27

Why are we commanded to make disciples of all nations?

All four of the Gospels conclude with Jesus giving a final commission to his disciples. These commissions are all given by Jesus Christ after the resurrection. They are given at different times and places throughout the forty days between his resurrection and his ascension. Each emphasizes different ways in which the church is called to bear witness to Christ between that time and his final return. In Matthew's gospel we are commanded to "make disciples of all nations." In Mark's gospel we are commanded to "preach the good news to every person in the whole world." In Luke's gospel we are commanded to be "his witnesses." Finally, in John's gospel we are "sent" by Christ just as Christ himself was sent into the world.

It becomes clear upon reflection that Jesus is giving the church four distinct ways to extend his mission into the world.

Some are called to the ministry of discipleship. Notice that Matthew does not merely say "disciple individuals," which is how we often interpret this passage. Instead, he calls us to disciple "the nations." This, of course, includes the important ministry of discipling individuals, but it also means that we have a responsibility to shape and instruct the entire life of a nation. Christianity is never only about individual faith and devotion. Christ has called us to manifest his glory in the whole life of a culture, including art, architecture, politics, education, social arrangements, family life, and so forth.

Mark's gospel reminds us of the special role of preaching or proclamation which has been given to the church. We often hear the phrase, attributed wrongly to St. Francis of Assisi, that we are to "preach the gospel at all times; use words if necessary." If this is taken to mean that we are to live out the gospel in our lives and deeds, then it is a noteworthy point worth remembering. But, it should never supplant the need for the gospel to be spoken and proclaimed in words to the entire world. The people of God have been given revelation and a message to share, and that must be articulated both in word and in deed.

Luke's gospel commands us to be "his witnesses." This implies the laying down of our lives for the sake of the gospel.

This does not only mean being willing to be a martyr for Jesus Christ, but includes all the ways that we "lay our lives down" for the sake of the gospel. It includes things which seem as mundane as giving up of our time to serve in a soup kitchen or volunteering to teach a Sunday school class. We are called to sacrificially give our lives and our gifts for the gospel in whatever way he leads us.

Finally, John's gospel reminds us that the church must be a sending church. We must send people forth to bear his message to the ends of the earth. We should support those who are called into full-time pastoring or mission work. The church needs these laborers and they are worthy of our support and encouragement. We all have resources which we are called to invest in Kingdom work, and we should freely offer those to Christ.

These commissions of Christ were not just meant for the original disciples; they are commissions for *all* disciples of Jesus Christ. We should never forget that we are all called to become full participants in his mission in the world, not merely performing tasks, but participating in extending his life, his Kingdom, and his purposes in the world. We should all see ourselves as joining *with* him in his mission, rather than as isolated individuals obeying commands. What a joy it is to know that, ultimately, he is the great redeemer and reconciler of the world. We have the privilege of sharing with him in this work of redemption.

Scripture Reading

Matthew 28:18–20
Mark 16:15–16
Luke 24:46–49

John 20:19–23
Acts 1:8
Acts 13:1–3

28

What is the bodily resurrection of the dead?

Christians believe in a bodily resurrection, we do not believe simply in a spiritual state where our souls live forever. Christianity affirms that our entire life is being redeemed, which includes our bodies, our minds, our souls, and our spirits. In fact, the apostle Paul is so determined to establish the Christian view of the resurrection body that he links the resurrection of our bodies in the future with the resurrection of Jesus Christ in the past. Paul teaches that if Christ has not been physically raised, then we also will not be raised. If Christ has not been raised, then we have no hope, we are to be pitied, we are still in our sins. In 1 Corinthians 15:16, Paul says, "for if the dead are not raised, then Christ has not been raised either."

The whole certainty of our faith in the general, bodily resurrection at the end of time is linked to the bodily resurrection of Jesus Christ. This is why the Apostles' Creed first declares, "on the third day he rose again from the dead," and then goes on to affirm that we believe in the "resurrection of the body." The Resurrection of Christ is the key and the foundation for our own resurrection from the dead.

In 1 Corinthians 15:20, Paul declares, "But Christ has indeed been raised from the dead, the firstfruits of those who have fallen asleep." Notice how he avoids the word "death" in regard to us, because that word has a finality to it; and in Christ, death does not have the final word. The Bible refers to the first death and the second death. The first death is the one we know about. It refers to the fact that our bodies are decaying and rushing towards the grave. One day you wake up and notice that you don't run up steps like you used to. You might notice some aches and pains which weren't there before. These are gentle reminders that our bodies in their present form are not built for eternity. We may dye our hair, watch our weight, or exercise vigorously, but we all know that our bodies in their present form are dying. Unless Christ returns in our lifetime, we will someday all physically die. This is the first death.

The Scriptures speak of a second death in Revelation 20:6. This refers to eternal death apart from Christ. For the believer in Christ, the second death has no power over us. Our sins have already been judged in Christ. They have been paid for through the power of the cross and we are not subject to eternal judgment. So, once that is removed, Paul doesn't even want to use the word "death" for us. He simply evokes a euphemism and says, "those who have fallen asleep." For us, our physical death is like falling asleep. In other words, it is like sleep in the sense that one day we will wake up to a new day, but not just any day—the Day of Resurrection.

Christians believe that our resurrected body will be a splendorous, glorious body. While there are continuities between our present body and the resurrected body, it is mostly a transformed body (1 Cor. 15:35–42). Paul likens it to a kernel of corn compared with the full stalk. This is far more than just a retooling of the body we have. This will not be like one of those famous "before" and "after" shots on a diet commercial. This is a splendorous transformation which we can hardly imagine.

> *The body that is sown is perishable, it is raised imperishable;*
> *It is sown in dishonor [sickness and sin], it is raised in glory;*
> *It is sown in weakness, it is raised in power;*
> *It is sown a natural body, it is raised a spiritual body.*

> —1 Corinthians 15:42–44

Your resurrection body will be imperishable, not subject to decay. It will be glorious. It will be powerful. It is called a "spiritual body," which brings together two words into one phrase—body and spirit. It is an unusual combination, but it is not a mere spiritual existence; it is a bodily existence which is constantly vivified and empowered through his spiritual life. We will live forever because our life is tied to his life, and since God cannot die, we will not die—but instead, will enjoy an everlasting life.

Scripture Reading

Luke 20:27–40

John 11:23–27

Romans 6:5

1 Corinthians 15:12–57

Philippians 3:10–11

Revelation 20:5–6

29

Why is Jesus returning to judge the world?

For many people, including Christians, the final judgment of God might appear to be incongruent with the God of grace, forgiveness, and love which we have seen so powerfully in the person and ministry of Jesus Christ. We often downplay the Scriptures about God's judgment or relegate the topic to the God of the Old Testament. However, this is not how the Bible portrays the theme of God's judgment. Rather, the judgment of God is the final vindication of God's righteousness. It is a good and glorious thing, for final judgment is the time when God will set all things right. Jesus himself spoke of it quite often right in the pages of the New Testament. This final vindication involves two main things.

First, Judgment Day will reveal and make known all sins. The secrets of everyone's heart will be revealed. Romans 2:16 says, "This will take place on the day when God will judge men's secrets." Every thought, every idle word, every deed—even deeds done in absolute secrecy—will be made known and laid bare. Jesus said in Luke 12:2-3 "there is nothing concealed that will not be disclosed, or hidden that will not be made known. What you have said in the dark will be heard in the daylight, and what you have whispered in the ear in the inner rooms will be proclaimed from the roofs." Crimes which people thought they had "gotten away with" will suddenly be known. All sins will be revealed and publicly exposed.

This is actually good news, because it means that everything will be "set right." We all know that the courts of human justice have severe limitations. There are crimes which never go punished, and there are crimes for which no human punishment seems fully adequate. This is why it does not make sense to say that God "would never judge anyone, he only forgives." Crucial to the biblical doctrine of God's love is that all things will eventually be made right. God's love for those who have been wronged, and God's love for righteousness and truth, are one and the same with his determination to set everything right in the end, which is what judgment is. A New Creation where wickedness was still allowed to flourish would not be a place in which we long to dwell. Love without justice is mere sentimentality.

Judgment at the end of time must be seen and understood in the larger context that God has taken upon himself, through Christ, the just sentence of judgment which sinners deserved. Jesus bore our sins on the cross. He accepted the full weight of the guilty verdict. Now, through the gospel, the entire world is invited to receive that gift of grace. Jesus has already borne the judgment of the entire world, and that is where the forgiveness and grace of God are made manifest. However, for those who do not accept Jesus Christ, they must stand before the bar of God's justice and render a full account of their own lives, receiving the due penalty for every thought or deed.

Second, Judgment Day will vindicate the faith of the church. Praise God that the record of sins is not the only book in heaven. There is another book which has a record of all those who have placed their faith in Jesus Christ. For the believer, Judgment Day is transformed from a day of fear and trial into a day of vindication and joy. The Scripture says that the name of that other book is known as the Lamb's Book of Life. That book will reveal the names of those people whose sins have already been paid for because we have trusted in the provision offered through the gospel of our Lord Jesus Christ.

The church will be vindicated, not because we are without sin, but because of our perseverance in faith. This is the truth celebrated in the song which says, "he paid a debt, he did not owe; I owed a debt, I could not pay; Christ Jesus came and washed my sins away!" The people of God will be rewarded for their faithfulness and it will be a day of great joy and celebration. In the Scriptures we do not see the people of God dreading the Day of Judgment. Rather, we see them praying for that day to come, and longing for the time when God will finally set all things right.

Scripture Reading

John 5:22

1 Corinthians 3:11–15

1 Thessalonians 4:13–18

2 Thessalonians 1:5–10

2 Timothy 4:1

Revelation 20:11–15

30

What is the ultimate goal and purpose of the people of God?

The ultimate goal and purpose of the people of God is nothing less than union with Christ himself. Earlier we explored the many facets of salvation which begin with God's prior action in extending prevenient grace to depraved sinners. This process continues through our justification, sanctification, and final glorification. However, the final goal of salvation is union with Christ. We will become like him and we will be united with his everlasting life.

This means that our long sojourn in life will finally culminate in our true home. We all know that there are homeless people in the world today. Our hearts go out to those who have no place to rest or to come home to at night. However, the Scripture understands that all of us are homeless in a deeper sense, even if we happen to live in a beautiful house. We recognize that we live in a world marred by sin and brokenness. No one can escape this, regardless of how we try to insulate ourselves from the pain and ravages of the world around us. We all know that even those who enjoy great comfort and plenty of money in this life are often marked by broken relationships and deep pain and bondage. As we get older we recognize that our bodies are not built to last forever, and despite the best health care in the world, we know that our days on this earth are numbered; we are but sojourners in this world.

Our earthly life, compared to eternity, is but a mere breath. In heaven, we are not only granted eternal life, but we are delivered from the very presence of sin. We will have a resurrected body which is eternally sustained by his life and vitality.

Eternal life is not the end of something, but the beginning of the positive work of building a world which is centered on God's glory. Since the Fall even our best work has been focused on redeeming a lost world and responding to the brokenness of the world. However, in the New Creation we will no longer live in a lost, broken, and fallen world. Instead, we can then move on to the positive work of ruling and reigning with Christ and doing the work which he originally called Adam and Even to at the dawn of creation. In this sense, the whole history of the world has been remedial work, getting us back to the starting point.

In the New Creation, as those who have been resurrected and glorified, we will be called to a new array of positive work and labor. All the creativity and energy and intellectual curiosity which has been so hampered by sin and the world's fallenness will be removed, and we will be set free to live and work in an abundance which we can now only imagine. People sometimes ask me if I think we will have computers in heaven. I don't know if we will, but I do know that if we need them we will build them, and they will be built in a way that even Steve Jobs with all his creativity and imagination could never comprehend. I don't know if we will have musical instruments or if we will write new scores of music. But if we do, then we will create instruments which we never thought possible, and new musical compositions will be written which will make Handel's *Messiah* seem like mere hors d'oeuvres of a great feast. In fact, it is probably an understatement to say that we will be starting back at the Garden of Eden. Even that is too small a vision of what is in store for us. The New Jerusalem will be far grander than even what Adam and Eve experienced in the garden prior to the fall.

The most important thing, however, will not be the streets of gold or the mansions he has prepared for us, or even the new work we are called to do. The greatest reality of the New Creation will be the never-ending presence of God. We are told that there will be no temple in the New Jerusalem. This is because the presence of God now fills the whole of life. The Scriptures tell us that in his presence there is fullness of joy and pleasures forevermore. What a grand and glorious future awaits us all!

Scripture Reading

Psalm 16:9–11
1 John 3:2
Revelation 21:1–22:6

HYMN

A Call to Learn

As with my previous devotional books, *Word Made Flesh: Reflections on the Incarnation*, *Christ the Fulfillment*, and *This We Believe! Meditations on the Apostles' Creed*, I have included an original hymn written by Julie Tennent. This is because Christian learning takes place in the context of worship, and as our minds reflect upon the truths of God, we are led more and more into the humble place of worship before him.

This hymn is taken from Isaiah 50:4–10, which is one of the great "servant songs" found in the book of Isaiah. The most familiar servant song is found in Isaiah 53, where we see a depiction of the Suffering Servant. In this servant song, however, we see the Servant of the Lord as one who is ready to be instructed and taught. The Lord's servant has an open ear and a willing heart to hear God's Word and to be instructed in his ways. The servant is eager to awaken every morning and "listen like one being taught"—and then to walk in trust, relying upon the Lord whom he has come to know.

Jesus Christ is the Great Servant, and we are called to his example of a well-instructed tongue and attentive ears, listening well to the Word of God. This, then, is a hymn for catechesis, calling us to be among God's servants who are eager to be instructed, to listen, and to learn.

Tune possibilities:
Ellacombe ("Hosanna, Loud Hosanna")
Kingsfold ("O Sing a Song of Bethlehem")
Materna ("O Beautiful, for Spacious Skies")
Forest Green ("I Sing the Mighty Power of God")

A Call to Learn

by Julie Tennent
Isaiah 50:4–10
Common meter: 86.86 double

The Servant of the Lord will have a well-instructed tongue,
to know the Word that only can sustain the weary one.
O Christ, great Servant of the Lord, awaken us each day
to listen with an open ear to all that You would say.

The Servant of the Lord will love in spite of trial or shame,
for he has set his face like flint to serve God's Holy name.
O Christ, great Servant of the Lord, You vindicate Your own;
help us to learn the Way of faith and trust in You alone.

The Servant of the Lord will walk within the Righteous Way,
will trust in God both in the dark and in the light of day.
O Christ, great Servant of the Lord, teach us each day to be
Awakened with an eager mind and heart to follow Thee!

APPENDIX A

Apostles' Creed

In 2011, I published a small book entitled *This We Believe! Meditations on the Apostles' Creed*, which (as the title suggests) contains a meditation on each of the phrases of the Apostles' Creed. It has been used by individuals, small groups, and entire churches around the country to understand basic Christian doctrine. It can also be used as a companion to this volume for home catechesis or confirmation classes in churches. The book is available at Amazon.com or www.seedbed.com.

Apostles' Creed

I believe in God, the Father Almighty, creator of heaven and earth,

I believe in Jesus Christ, His only Son, our Lord,

who was conceived by the Holy Spirit, born of the Virgin Mary,

suffered under Pontius Pilate; was crucified, died and was buried.

He descended to the dead.

The third day he rose again from the dead.

He ascended into heaven and sits at the right hand of God the Father Almighty.

From there, He shall come to judge the living and the dead.

I believe in the Holy Spirit,

the holy catholic Church, the communion of saints,

the forgiveness of sins,

the resurrection of the body, and the life everlasting.

APPENDIX B

Ten Commandments

1. You shall have no other gods before me.
2. You shall not make for yourself an idol.
3. You shall not misuse the name of the Lord your God.
4. Remember the Sabbath day by keeping it holy.
5. Honor your father and your mother.
6. You shall not murder.
7. You shall not commit adultery.
8. You shall not steal.
9. You shall not give false testimony against your neighbor.
10. You shall not covet your neighbor's house.

APPENDIX C

The Lord's Prayer

Our Father who art in heaven, hallowed be Thy name.
Thy kingdom come, Thy will be done on earth as it is in
heaven. Give us this day our daily bread and forgive us our
trespasses as we have forgiven those who trespass against us.
And lead us not into temptation, but deliver us from evil,
for Thine is the kingdom and the power and the glory,
forever and ever. Amen.

About the Author

Dr. Timothy Tennent received his M.Div. in 1984 from Gordon-Conwell; the Th.M. in Ecumenics, with a focus on Islam from Princeton Theological Seminary; and did graduate work in linguistics (TESL) at the University of Georgia. He completed his Ph.D. in Non-western Christianity with a focus on Hinduism and Indian Christianity in 1998 at the University of Edinburgh in Scotland. He served eleven years as professor of World Missions and Indian Studies at Gordon-Conwell Theological Seminary in South Hamilton, Massachusetts. He has ministered and taught in China, Thailand, Nigeria, Eastern Europe, and India. Ordained in the United Methodist Church, he has pastored churches in Georgia, and preached regularly in churches throughout New England and across the country.

In 2009, Dr. Tennent was inaugurated as the eighth president of Asbury Theological Seminary. In addition to his service as president of the Seminary and professor of World Christianity, he is author to a growing collection of books and publications on missions and global Christianity. He also serves on the faculty of Luther W. New Jr. Theological College of Dehra Dun, India where he has taught annually since 1989.

Visit TimothyTennent.com to follow Dr. Tennent's blog,
listen to his sermons, and further connect with his work.
Follow him on Twitter @timtennent.